Commissioned by St Paul's School, Brooklandville,
Maryland, for the dedication of the Schoenstein Organ
in St Paul's Chapel on 10 November 2002

Toccata

GERRE HANCOCK

I: Foundations 8', 4', III/I, II/I
II: Foundations 8', 4', III/II
III: Foundations 8', 4', Reeds 8'
Ped.: Foundations 16', 8', III/Ped., II/Ped.